ODD BODS

To Trudy and Elena, my special "Odd Buds"

Millbrook Press™
An imprint of Lerner Publishing Group, Inc.
241 First Avenue North
Minneapolis, MN 55401 USA

For reading levels and more information, look up this title at www.lernerbooks.com.

Designed by Kimberly Morales.
Main body text set in Mikado.
Typeface provided by HVD Fonts.

Library of Congress Cataloging-in-Publication Data

Names: Murphy, Julie, 1965– author.
Title: Odd bods : the world's unusual animals / by Julie Murphy.
Description: Minneapolis, MN : Millbrook Press, [2021] | Includes bibliographical references. | Audience: Ages 4–9 (provided by Millbrook Press.) | Audience: Grades 2–3 (provided by Millbrook Press.) | Description based on print version record and CIP data provided by publisher; resource not viewed.
Identifiers: LCCN 2019047349 (print) | LCCN 2019047350 (ebook) | ISBN 9781728401539 (ebook) | ISBN 9781541585027 (library binding)
Subjects: LCSH: Animals—Adaptation—Juvenile literature.
Classification: LCC QH546 (ebook) | LCC QH546 .M87 2021 (print) | DDC 591—dc23

LC record available at https://lccn.loc.gov/2019047349
LC record available at https://lccn.loc.gov/2019047350

Manufactured in the United States of America
1-47377-47998-7/7/2020

ODD BODS

The World's Unusual Animals

Julie Murphy

Ⓜ Millbrook Press / Minneapolis

Odd boas don't look like most animals—and that's what makes them great! They might have spiky heads, extra-long fingers, or big, huge noses. But did you know that their odd features also make them super survivors?

A sharp spike can help you hide!

The **thorn bug** lives on prickly plants, so looking like a thorn helps this bug to stay hidden from hungry predators. And any animal that sees through the disguise might think twice before swallowing this spike!

A big, broad snout can be
fantastic for feeding!

The **dugong** uses its sensitive, bristly snout to snuffle up seagrass. In warm, shallow sea meadows, dugongs chomp seagrass day and night. That's why they are also known as *sea cows*!

Bright red lips can help you to stand out from the crowd!

This remarkable mouth may help the **red-lipped batfish** be seen by others of its kind. In the dim light on the seafloor, red lips can act like a signal, telling future mates, *Hey look! I'm over here!*

An extra-long middle finger can make you a **first-rate food finder!**

Tap, tap, tap. The longest finger of the **aye-aye** hits against the tree. The sound of the echo tells this lemur where insects are hiding under the bark. Its teeth rip the bark open. Then that long finger gets to work again, plucking out the tasty reward.

Big teeth can be useful for digging a home!

The **naked mole rat** uses its long front teeth to dig a vast underground burrow. It's usually not very cold belowground, so the mole rat doesn't need fur. For rare chilly snaps, this wrinkly rodent huddles with its large family. Who doesn't love a cuddle every once in a while?

Stinging fingers can
keep you from being eaten!

The **glaucus sea slug** uses stingers in
its fingerlike branches to capture and eat tiny
stinging animals. Then it stores the stingers in
its branches to put off its own predators!

Spines and scales can get you a drink in the desert!

On cold desert nights, dew forms on the **thorny devil**. The next morning, the dew trickles down the lizard's spines and flows along tiny grooves between its scales. All these mini rivers lead to the mouth and a refreshing drink.

A long, pointy tusk can be an awesome weapon!

A male **narwhal** sometimes uses its tusk to fight in duels. Perhaps it is fighting over females. Narwhals also knock small fish senseless before eating them. What a wacky way to go fishing!

A hefty, hooked beak and
scary stare can be
fierce features!

The **shoebill**, with its intense gaze, spots prey. Then the shoebill's powerful beak grabs it. This bold bird is one mean feeder. It eats almost anything in the swamp: fish, frogs, snakes, lizards, rats, and even other waterbirds!

Frills can help you blend in with the background!

The frilly disguise of the **leafy sea dragon** helps it to hide from unfriendly eyes. Swaying in the current helps it blend in even more. It's hard to tell this sea dragon from seaweed!

A nose like this can keep you sneeze-free in summer and warmer in winter!

The oversized nose of the **saiga antelope** filters out dust during the hot, dry summer. And in winter, its nose warms the freezing air the saiga antelope breathes in so its insides don't get too cold.

While the **Odd Bods** have features that look freaky, they are also very useful! Whether it's finding a mate or finding food, avoiding predators, or making a home, Odd Bods' unique traits make each animal a winner in its own wonderful way.

MORE ODD FACTS

Thorn Bug

Scientific name: *Umbonia crassicornis*
Type: insect
Home/distribution: Central and South America, Mexico, and introduced in southern Florida
Habitat: tropical forests
Diet: the sap inside the stems of young trees
Life span: three months
Lifestyle: arboreal (lives in trees)
Size: about 0.5 inches (1.3 cm)
Conservation status: Unknown (not assessed)
Fun fact: Thorn bugs use their supersharp beaks to bite into plants and suck up the sap like a milkshake.
Bonus activity! Hear a thorn bug call: http://www.libraries -of-life.org/invertnet-collection-network-the-thorn-bug.html.

Dugong

Scientific name: *Dugong dugon*
Type: mammal
Home/distribution: coastal ocean waters around East Africa, Southeast Asia, and Oceania
Habitat: tropical, shallow, marine waters near coastlines
Diet: seagrass
Life span: seventy-plus years
Lifestyle: nomadic (moves around many different places)
Size: 7.9 to 13 feet (2.4 to 4 m) long
Conservation status: Vulnerable
Fun fact: Dugongs may have inspired sailors to create the very first mermaid stories.

Red-Lipped Batfish (or Galapagos Batfish)

Scientific name: *Ogcocephalus darwini*
Type: fish
Home/distribution: southeastern Pacific Ocean, around the Galápagos Islands, and as far south as Peru
Habitat: marine reefs, near coast, with a sandy bottom
Diet: mollusks and small invertebrates
Life span: unknown
Lifestyle: benthic (lives on the seafloor)
Size: 7.9 inches (20 cm)
Conservation status: Least Concern
Fun fact: The red-lipped batfish can hardly swim! It prefers to walk on its footlike fins on the seafloor.

Aye-Aye

Scientific name: *Daubentonia madagascariensis*
Type: mammal
Home/distribution: Madagascar
Habitat: tropical forests and shrubland
Diet: seeds, fruit, nuts, sap, and insect larvae
Life span: twenty-three years (in captivity)
Lifestyle: nocturnal (awake at night), arboreal (lives in trees), and solitary (lives alone)
Size: 14 to 17 inches (36 to 44 cm) tall
Conservation status: Endangered
Fun fact: As the aye-aye moves among the trees at night in its forest home, its big ears listen for danger, wide-apart eyes keep watch, and that big, bushy tail helps with balance.

Naked Mole Rat

Scientific name: *Heterocephalus glaber*
Type: mammal
Home/distribution: East Africa (Djibouti, Ethiopia, Somalia, and Kenya)
Habitat: underground tunnels in dry grasslands and in shrublands
Diet: roots and other underground parts of plants such as tubers
Life span: an average of thirty years in the wild
Lifestyle: mostly subterranean (lives underground), colonial (lives in large family groups), and polyandry (one queen who has most of the babies)
Size: 5.8 to 6.5 inches (15 to 17 cm) long
Conservation status: Least Concern
Fun fact: The naked mole rat's tiny eyes can barely see. But that doesn't matter in a pitch-black burrow. It has sensitive hairs along its body that work like whiskers to feel the way.

Glaucus

Scientific name: *Glaucus atlanticus*
Type: sea slug (invertebrate), which is a type of mollusk (includes clams, snails, slugs, squid, and octopuses)
Home/distribution: temperate and tropical waters around the world
Habitat: marine, coastal, and tropical
Diet: jellyfish
Life span: unknown
Lifestyle: floats upside down on top of the sea
Size: 1.6 inches (4 cm) long
Conservation status: Unknown (not assessed)
Fun fact: The glaucus blows an air bubble and swallows it so it can spend its life floating on the waves upside down!

Thorny Devil

Scientific name: *Moloch horridus*
Type: reptile (lizard)
Home/distribution: dry parts of Australia
Habitat: desert and dry shrubland with sandy soils
Diet: ants
Life span: six to twenty years in the wild
Lifestyle: terrestrial (lives on the ground)
Size: 3 to 4.3 inches (7.6 to 11 cm) long
Conservation status: Least Concern
Fun fact: Thorny devils walk in a slow, jerky, backward-and-forward motion. This weird walk may confuse predators.

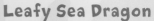

Narwhal

Scientific name: *Monodon monoceros*

Type: mammal

Home/distribution: the Arctic Ocean, including northeastern Canada, northern Greenland, Svalbard, and northern Russia

Habitat: marine

Diet: fish, squid, and shrimp

Life span: thirty to fifty-five years in the wild

Lifestyle: gregarious (lives in groups of six to twenty animals)

Size: 157 to 185 inches (400 to 470 cm) long

Conservation status: Least Concern

Fun fact: Male narwhals have two teeth. The tooth on the right usually stays small. The left one usually becomes the long tusk, which can grow longer than a Ping-Pong table!

Shoebill

Scientific name: *Balaeniceps rex*

Type: bird

Home/distribution: east-central Africa

Habitat: wetlands

Diet: fish, frogs, water snakes, young crocodiles, rats, mice, and young birds

Life span: around thirty-five years in the wild

Lifestyle: usually sedentary (stays in one place) and solitary (lives alone)

Size: 43 to 55 inches (110 to 140 cm) tall

Conservation status: Vulnerable

Fun fact: For the first ten weeks of their lives, shoebill chicks topple over when they try to stand because their beaks are too big for their bodies!

Leafy Sea Dragon

Scientific name: *Phycodurus eques*

Type: fish

Home/distribution: off southern Australia

Habitat: marine, seagrass meadows, seaweed beds, and rocky reefs 16 to 49 feet (5 to 15 m) deep, where seaweeds such as kelp grow

Diet: shrimp and other small crustaceans

Life span: unknown in the wild (two to three years in aquariums)

Lifestyle: moves slowly through water as it mimics seaweed, quietly approaching prey

Size: up to 14 inches (35 cm) long

Conservation status: Least Concern but Near Threatened

Fun fact: The male sea dragon holds his mate's eggs against his tail for four to six weeks. After the eggs hatch, he releases the tiny hatchlings into the sea.

Saiga Antelope

Scientific name: *Saiga tatarica*

Type: mammal

Home/distribution: eastern Europe (Russia, Mongolia, and Kazakhstan)

Habitat: open, dry grassland and desert

Diet: grasses and herbs

Life span: an average of ten to twelve years in the wild

Lifestyle: nomadic (moves around different places), migratory (seasonally moving from one place to another), and herding (lives in a group of thousands)

Size: about 1.9 to 2.6 feet (0.6 to 0.8 m) tall and 3.2 to 4.9 feet (1 to 1.5 m) long

Conservation status: Critically Endangered

Fun fact: Can you believe it? The male saiga antelope's already supersized nose swells even larger in the breeding season!

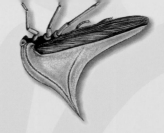

EXPLORE MORE

Books

Ghigna, Charles. *Strange, Unusual, Gross & Cool Animals*. New York: Liberty Street, 2016.

Grodzicki, Jenna. *I See Sea Food: Sea Creatures That Look Like Food*. Minneapolis: Millbrook Press, 2019.

Hearst, Michael. *Unusual Creatures: A Mostly Accurate Account of Earth's Strangest Animals*. San Francisco: Chronicle, 2012.

Stewart, Melissa. *Pipsqueaks, Slowpokes, and Stinkers*. Atlanta: Peachtree, 2018.

Websites

National Geographic Kids: The Ocean's Weirdest Creatures
https://www.natgeokids.com/uk/discover/animals/sea-life/strange-sea-creatures/
Learn more about oceanic odd bods at this website.

Science Kids: Animal Facts
http://www.sciencekids.co.nz/sciencefacts/animals.html
Can you find some more odd bods? Take a look at this site to learn interesting animal facts.

PHOTO ACKNOWLEDGMENTS

Image credits: DeAgostini/Getty Images, pp. 1, 2, 31, 32; Neil Bromhall/Shutterstock.com, p. 3; Natphotos/Photodisc/Getty Images, p. 4; Alastair Pollock Photography/Getty Images, p. 5 (top); RGB Ventures/Alamy Stock Photo, p. 5 (bottom); Ed Reschke/Getty Images, pp. 6–7; vkilikov/Shutterstock.com, pp. 8–9; Reinhard Dirscherl/Getty Images, pp. 10–11; Martin Lindsay/Alamy Stock Photo, pp. 12–13; Science Source/Getty Images, pp. 14–15; Sahara Frost/Shutterstock.com, pp. 16–17; Chris Watson/Getty Images, pp. 18–19; A & J Visage/Alamy Stock Photo, pp. 20–21; Sandra L. Grimm/Getty Images, pp. 22–23, 28; Shin Okamoto/Getty Images, pp. 24–25; Nikolay Denisov/Alamy Stock Photo, pp. 26–27; Laura Westlund/Independent Picture Service, p. 29. Background: GoodStudio/Shutterstock.com.

Cover: National Geographic Image Collection/Alamy Stock Photo. Back cover: David Haring/DUPC/Oxford Scientific/Getty Images; Reinhard Dirscherl/Getty Images; Ed Reschke/Getty Images. Jacket flap: guenterguni/E+/Getty Images. Background: GoodStudio/Shutterstock.com.